WORLD CUP RUGBY

To Graeme and Gill
at Publicity & Media

WORLD CUP RUGBY

Colin M. Jarman

Illustrated by Harry Venning

Hodder
Children's
Books

a division of Hodder Headline plc

Text copyright © Colin M. Jarman 1999
Illustrations copyright © Harry Venning 1999

The right of Colin M. Jarman and Harry Venning to be identified
as the author and illustrator of the Work has been asserted by them
in accordance with the Copyright, Designs and Patents Act 1988.

Published by Hodder Children's Books 1999

10 9 8 7 6 5 4 3 2 1

ISBN 0 340 75414 1

Printed by The Guernsey Press Co. Ltd.,
Guernsey, Channel Islands

Hodder Children's Books
A division of Hodder Headline plc
338 Euston Road
London NW1 3BH

CONTENTS

Welcome to the Rugby World Cup   6

Tournament Schedule and Rules   10

Results and Tables   11

World Cup Grounds   16

The Qualifying Process   18

How the Teams Qualified   19

The Qualifiers   35

Previous World Cups   76

Past World Cup Masters   86

Were you Paying Attention?   93

Make your own Rugby World
   Cup Predictions   94

Select your Dream Team   96

WELCOME TO THE RUGBY WORLD CUP

Like the soccer and cricket World Cups, the rugby union World Cup is held every four years.

In 1999, the rugby World Cup tournament will be staged for only the fourth time. Sixty-six teams were involved in a long and complicated qualifying process that started more than three years ago. Twenty teams are now left to compete in the Finals.

The opening game, on Friday 1 October, will take place in the newly completed Millennium Stadium in Cardiff, Wales. The hosts will take on the top team from the Americas - Argentina. Forty more games will then be played at the major Rugby union grounds throughout the British Isles and France as well as at smaller club grounds. The final will take place in Cardiff on Saturday 6 November.

In the previous three World Cup competitions, the trophy has been won by New Zealand, Australia and South Africa. Will one of them take the trophy home for a second time, or will a European team win it this time?

How will the host nation, Wales, fare?

Will one of the outsiders cause an upset by defeating one of the more fancied teams?

The answers to all these questions will come only as the games are played. You will find everything else you need to know about the rugby World Cup – its history, the complicated qualification process, the teams and players taking part and masses of other fascinating information – inside this book.

In addition, there is a quick quiz to test your knowledge and the opportunity to predict the group winners, the semi-finalists and, most importantly, the eventual winners. When the World Cup is over, turn to the back page of this book and select your own 'dream team'.

THE GAME OF RUGBY

It is now part of sporting legend that, during a game of soccer at Rugby School in 1823, a senior pupil 'with a fine disregard for the rules of football, as played in his time, first took the ball in his arms and ran with it, thus originating the distinctive feature of the rugby game'. A lot has changed since those early days of rugby, most notably the split between amateur and professional status in 1895 when clubs in the north of England formed their own Northern Union, later to become the Rugby League.

In rugby union, points are scored in four ways: by touching the ball down behind the goal line for a try (worth five points) and by three types of kick – a conversion (worth two points), a penalty and a drop goal (each worth three points).

There are 15 players on each side. They play in a very tightly organised system, with eight forwards and seven backs. You can see how they line up in the diagram below.

Rugby union positions

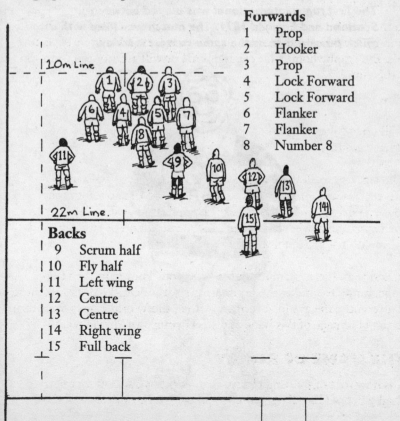

Forwards

1	Prop
2	Hooker
3	Prop
4	Lock Forward
5	Lock Forward
6	Flanker
7	Flanker
8	Number 8

Backs

9	Scrum half
10	Fly half
11	Left wing
12	Centre
13	Centre
14	Right wing
15	Full back

Until the early 1990s, when rugby union players were allowed to become professional, the amateur status of rugby union was always strictly adhered to, especially by those governing the sport. It was thought that the introduction of a World Cup competition would lead to players becoming professional, something that rugby's governing bodies wanted to avoid. In the 1950s, they even passed a law that forbade the creation of a World Cup.

The increasing worldwide interest in rugby, and the huge amounts of money that were made by promoting the game on television, eventually led to the obvious conclusion. More than 50 years after the first staging of soccer's World Cup, and 15 years after the first cricket World Cup, the first rugby union World Cup was held in 1987.

STATS 'N' STUFF

The first rugby international was played between Scotland and England 1871. The match was filled with as much passion then as the same contest is today.

THE WILLIAM WEBB ELLIS TROPHY

Whether the event at Rugby School actually took place is now open to question, since games similar to rugby and all its different variations have been played around the world for thousands of years. That does not really matter because the legend lives on, and the magnificent trophy presented to the winners of the rugby World Cup bears the name of that pupil – William Webb Ellis.

The trophy itself was originally made in 1906 by Garrards, the world-famous jewellers. It was altered slightly when it was purchased by the rugby World Cup committee in 1986.

Standing 38cm high, it is made from sterling silver gilded in gold. It has two handles, one shaped as a satyr's head and the other as a nymph's head. The trophy is decorated with bearded masks, lion masks and vine tendrils.

STATS 'N' STUFF

The William Webb Ellis Trophy is based on an original design for a trophy made by the famous French silversmith Paul de Lamerie in about 1740 – almost a century before William Webb Ellis picked up a soccer ball.

TOURNAMENT SCHEDULE AND RULES

Following the opening match at the Millennium Stadium in Cardiff on 1 October, another 29 group matches will be played at grounds throughout the British Isles and France. Then another nine knock-out matches will decide who will compete in the third place play-off and, of course in the final itself, back in Cardiff on 6 November.

The 20 teams have been divided into five pools of four. Each team will play three initial matches and will be awarded three points for a win, two points for a draw, and one point for a loss. Only the overall pool winners will automatically proceed to the quarter-finals. The five runners-up, together with the best third-placed team from the five pools, will play in an intermediate knock-out round on 20 October for the other three places in the quarter-finals.

The best third-placed team will be decided by a count-back system involving the number of tries scored, the number of points scored and conceded and, if necessary, the number of players sent off.

The three knock-out winners will join the pool winners in the quarter-finals, which will be played on 23 and 24 October. The four winners will progress to the semis at Twickenham near London on 30 and 31 October, and then the last two will play in the final in Cardiff on 6 November.

A full list of fixtures, together with dates and grounds, is given on the next few pages. There is space for you to fill in the results as they happen.

At the back of the book, there are pages where you can fill in your predictions before the championships start.

RESULTS AND TABLES

POOL A   All games to be played in Scotland

2 Oct	Galashiels	SPAIN	_____	URUGUAY	_____
3 Oct	Edinburgh	SCOTLAND	_____	S. AFRICA	_____
8 Oct	Edinburgh	SCOTLAND	_____	URUGUAY	_____
10 Oct	Edinburgh	S. AFRICA	_____	SPAIN	_____
15 Oct	Glasgow	S. AFRICA	_____	URUGUAY	_____
16 Oct	Edinburgh	SCOTLAND	_____	SPAIN	_____

Final table

TEAM	P	W	L	D	F	A	Pts
1 _____	__	__	__	__	__	__	__
2 _____	__	__	__	__	__	__	__
3 _____	__	__	__	__	__	__	__
4 _____	__	__	__	__	__	__	__

POOL B   All games to be played in England

2 Oct	Twickenham	ENGLAND	_____	ITALY	_____
3 Oct	Bristol	N. ZEALAND	_____	TONGA	_____
9 Oct	Twickenham	ENGLAND	_____	N. ZEALAND	_____
10 Oct	Leicester	ITALY	_____	TONGA	_____
14 Oct	Huddersfield	N. ZEALAND	_____	ITALY	_____
15 Oct	Twickenham	ENGLAND	_____	TONGA	_____

Final table

TEAM	P	W	L	D	F	A	Pts
1 _____	__	__	__	__	__	__	__
2 _____	__	__	__	__	__	__	__
3 _____	__	__	__	__	__	__	__
4 _____	__	__	__	__	__	__	__

POOL C   All games to be played in France

1 Oct	Beziers	FIJI	_____	NAMIBIA	_____
2 Oct	Beziers	FRANCE	_____	CANADA	_____
8 Oct	Bordeaux	FRANCE	_____	NAMIBIA	_____
9 Oct	Bordeaux	FIJI	_____	CANADA	_____
14 Oct	Toulouse	CANADA	_____	NAMIBIA	_____
16 Oct	Toulouse	FRANCE	_____	FIJI	_____

Final table

TEAM	P	W	L	D	F	A	Pts
1 _____	_	_	_	_	_	_	_
2 _____	_	_	_	_	_	_	_
3 _____	_	_	_	_	_	_	_
4 _____	_	_	_	_	_	_	_

POOL D   All games to be played in Wales

1 Oct	Cardiff	WALES	_____	ARGENTINA	_____
3 Oct	Wrexham	W. SAMOA	_____	JAPAN	_____
9 Oct	Cardiff	WALES	_____	JAPAN	_____
10 Oct	Llanelli	ARGENTINA	_____	W. SAMOA	_____
14 Oct	Cardiff	WALES	_____	W.SAMOA	_____
16 Oct	Cardiff	ARGENTINA	_____	JAPAN	_____

Final table

TEAM	P	W	L	D	F	A	Pts
1 _____	_	_	_	_	_	_	_
2 _____	_	_	_	_	_	_	_
3 _____	_	_	_	_	_	_	_
4 _____	_	_	_	_	_	_	_

POOL E   All games to be played in Ireland

2 Oct	Dublin	IRELAND	_____	USA	_____
3 Oct	Belfast	AUSTRALIA	_____	ROMANIA	_____
9 Oct	Dublin	USA	_____	ROMANIA	_____
10 Oct	Dublin	IRELAND	_____	AUSTRALIA	_____
14 Oct	Limerick	AUSTRALIA	_____	USA	_____
15 Oct	Dublin	IRELAND	_____	ROMANIA	_____

Final table

TEAM	P	W	L	D	F	A	Pts
1 _____	_	_	_	_	_	_	___
2 _____	_	_	_	_	_	_	___
3 _____	_	_	_	_	_	_	___
4 _____	_	_	_	_	_	_	___

PLAY-OFFS

20 Oct Twickenham

A Runners-up Pool B   Runners-up Pool C

_____ _____   _____ _____

20 Oct Edinburgh

B Runners-up Pool A   Runners-up Pool D

_____ _____   _____ _____

20 Oct Lens

C Runners-up Pool D   Best third-placed

_____ _____   _____ _____

QUARTER-FINALS

23 Oct Cardiff

W   Winners Group D   Winners Group E

_____ _____   _____ _____

24 Oct Paris

X   Winners Group A   Winners Play-off A

_____ _____   _____ _____

24 Oct Edinburgh

Y   Winners Group C   Winners Play-off B

_____ _____   _____ _____

24 Oct Dublin

Z   Winners Group B   Winners Play-off C

_____ _____   _____ _____

SEMI-FINALS

30 Oct   Winners Q-final W   Winners Q-final X
Twickenham
                   _____ _____   _____ _____

31 Oct   Winners Q-final Y   Winners Q-final Z
Twickenham
                   _____ _____   _____ _____

THIRD PLACE PLAY-OFF

4 Nov   _____ _____   _____ _____
Cardiff

1999 WORLD CUP FINAL

6 Nov
Cardiff

Tries

Conversions

Penalties

Drop goals

My Man of the Match: _____

WORLD CUP GROUNDS

The 41 matches will be played at 18 venues – five in France, four in England and three each in Scotland, Ireland and Wales. Here is a brief guide to some of the stadiums that will be used.

MILLENNIUM STADIUM – Cardiff, Wales
Newly built to replace the old Cardiff Arms Park, this state-of-the-art stadium has a capacity of 72,500. In addition to hosting the opening and closing ceremonies, the final and the third place play-off, five other games will be played at the Millennium Stadium, making it the most used venue of the tournament.

TWICKENHAM – London, England
Rebuilt in stages over the past decade, the true home of world rugby now boasts a superb three-tiered stand capable of accommodating 73,000 fans. For the 1999 World Cup, both semi-finals will be staged here, as well as four other matches.

MURRAYFIELD – Edinburgh, Scotland
Like most other grounds in Great Britain, Scotland's rugby headquarters has undergone a major transformation in the past decade, turning it into a modern all-seater, all-weather stadium with a capacity of 67,500. Four pool matches will be played here plus one of the play-offs and a quarter-final.

LANSDOWNE ROAD – Dublin, Ireland
The home of Irish rugby, Lansdowne Road is one of the oldest rugby grounds in the world. Built in 1878, it has a capacity of 49,250. Four group matches will be here and one of the quarter-finals.

STADE DE FRANCE – Paris, France
Built for the 1998 soccer World Cup Finals, this multi-purpose stadium is now the home of French rugby. With a capacity of 78,500, it is the largest venue to be used for the rugby World Cup, but only one game, a quarter-final, is scheduled to be played here.

The other 13 grounds are:
Wales
Stradey Park, Llanelli (capacity 13,600)
The Racecourse Ground, Wrexham (capacity 11,250)
England
Ashton Gate, Bristol (capacity 22,000)
McAlpine Stadium, Huddersfield (capacity 24,000)
Welford Road, Leicester (capacity 16,000)
France
Stade Municipal, Toulouse (capacity 37,500)
Stade Felix Bollaert, Lens (capacity 42,000)

Stade Mediterannée, Beziers (capacity 20,000)
Stade Lescure, Bordeaux (capacity 36,000)

Ireland
Ravenhill Park, Belfast (capacity 11,700)
Thomond Park, Limerick (capacity 13,300)

Scotland
Netherdale, Galashiels (capacity 10,000)
Hampden Park, Glasgow (capacity 55,000)

THE QUALIFYING PROCESS

In 1996, when the rugby World Cup committee sat down to work out the structure for the 1999 World Cup Finals, they had two new ideas that they wanted to include in the format. They wanted to give more minor rugby-playing nations the chance to compete at the highest level, and they wanted to increase the number of countries in the Finals from 16 to 20. To achieve this, a qualifying system was adopted that was so complex and drawn out that even the most avid rugby supporter was confused by the number of games that would be played.

The actual qualifying system would involve the weaker nations playing-off against each other in zonal rounds to earn the right to compete against better and stronger teams. It was decided that six teams should qualify from Europe, three teams from the Americas and Pacific regions, and one team from each of the African and Asian regions, to give 14 qualifiers. The next-best seven teams from the regions and zones would be given a chance to earn one of two places in the Finals, by going into a final qualification stage, or repêchage. The top three teams from 1995 – South Africa, New Zealand and France – were pre-selected, along with Wales as host nation, making 20 teams altogether. The other big-guns, such as Australia, England, Scotland and Ireland would join the competition for the 16 qualification places in the later stages.

HOW THE TEAMS QUALIFIED

The first qualifying game was played three years before the official Finals were to be held, in September 1996 in the Baltic city of Riga. The home country, Latvia, easily defeated Norway 44-6. Since then, games have been played in all parts of the world in cities such as Oslo, Budapest, Lisbon, Brussels and Vienna in Europe; Nairobi and Casablanca in Africa; Santiago, Buenos Aires and Montevideo in South America; Singapore, Kuala Lumpur and Bangkok in Asia. Around the Pacific Ocean, the venues took on an exotic feel, with games being staged in places such as Rarotonga, Papeeta, and Nuku'Alofa.

Since 1996, there have been many outstanding performances, including some that broke scoring records. There have also been some truly surprising results, especially involving the smaller nations, such as Andorra and the Arabian Gulf, who headed their first-round groups despite having only 600 players between them!

All the results and league tables are shown on the next few pages, in a format that, we hope, will make the very complicated system slightly easier to understand.

African Zone

South Africa, by far the most powerful rugby-playing nation on the continent, qualified as champions, so the African zone matches were closely fought. The first matches were played in April 1997, with the Arabian Gulf team, chosen from just eight clubs in various countries in and around the Gulf, astounding everyone by beating Botswana (53-13) and Zambia (44-30) to win the round.

The Arabian Gulf was joined in round B by Kenya and Tunisia. Each team won one game but Tunisia was awarded top spot because they had scored more tries, most of them in the 52-5 win over Kenya. In the next round, Tunisia, Namibia and Zimbabwe again recorded one win each. This time, Tunisia failed to reach the next stage on count-back, despite a fine 20-17 win over Namibia.

In the final round, all the matches were played in Casablanca, Morocco in September 1998. The much-fancied Ivory Coast, which had qualified for the 1995 World Cup, failed to register a single win. Namibia, which had finished behind Zimbabwe in the previous round, won all three games to go straight into the Finals.

Amazingly, in the three games played, Namibia conceded just 32 points, whereas in the previous round against inferior opposition they had conceded 46 points in just two games. Morocco won two close-fought matches (15-9 against Zimbabwe and 6-3 against Ivory Coast) to finish in second place and earn a place in the repêchage stage held in early 1999.

AFRICAN ZONE TABLES

	P	W	L	D	F	A	Pts
ROUND A							
ARABIAN GULF	2	2	0	0	97	43	6
ZAMBIA	2	1	1	0	50	57	4
BOTSWANA	2	0	2	0	26	73	2

Arabian Gulf qualify for round B.

ROUND B

TUNISIA	2	1	1	0	63	17	4
KENYA	2	1	1	0	49	70	4
ARABIAN GULF	2	1	1	0	30	48	4

Tunisia qualify for round C having scored more tries.

ROUND C

ZIMBABWE	2	1	1	0	69	32	4
NAMIBIA	2	1	1	0	49	46	4
TUNISIA	2	1	1	0	29	60	4

Zimbabwe and Namibia qualify for round D having scored more tries.

ROUND D

NAMIBIA	3	3	0	0	78	32	9
MOROCCO	3	2	1	0	29	29	7
ZIMBABWE	3	1	2	0	55	54	5
IVORY COAST	3	0	3	0	13	60	3

Namibia qualify for the Finals.

Morocco qualify
for the repêchage.

American Zone

North and South America boast three good rugby-playing nations in Argentina, Canada and USA. All have qualified for every World Cup to date and this history meant that three qualifying spots were available from this zone.

In spite of the fact that there were only 12 teams taking part, four rounds were needed with the first round split into two pools of three teams. Guyana pulled out at the last minute leaving Trinidad & Tobago and Brazil to play a one-match decider, which Trinidad & Tobago easily won 41-0. In the other first round pool, Bermuda defeated the Bahamas 24-3 and swamped Barbados 52-3.

In round B, Chile joined the two zone winners and easily qualified for the next stage with high-scoring wins of 65-8 against Bermuda and 35-6 against Trinidad & Tobago. In round C, Chile lost 14-20 to Uruguay, and Paraguay barely put up any resistance to finish a very poor last.

Uruguay went on to compete with the 'Big Three' – Argentina, Canada and USA – all of whom qualified as expected. Argentina were the strongest and had three easy wins: 52-24 against USA; 55-0 against Uruguay; 54-28 against Canada.

The closest match of the entire American zone came in what was effectively the play-off for the last automatic Finals place. The United States only just beat Uruguay 21-16 to claim third place in the group, leaving Uruguay the consolation of a repêchage place.

AMERICAN ZONE TABLES

	P	W	L	D	F	A	Pts
ROUND A – Pool I							
TRINIDAD & Tobago	1	1	0	0	41	0	3
BRAZIL	1	0	1	0	0	41	1
GUYANA	Withdrew from competition						

Trinidad & Tobago qualify for round B.

ROUND A – Pool 2

BERMUDA	2	2	0	0	76	6	6
BAHAMAS	2	1	1	0	40	47	4
BARBADOS	2	0	2	0	26	89	2

Bermuda qualify for round B.

ROUND B

CHILE	2	2	0	0	113	14	6
BERMUDA	2	1	1	0	60	74	4
TRINIDAD	2	0	2	0	12	87	2

Chile qualify for round C.

ROUND C

URUGUAY	2	2	0	0	63	17	6
CHILE	2	1	1	0	68	26	4
PARAGUAY	2	0	2	0	9	97	2

Uruguay qualify for round D.

ROUND D

ARGENTINA	3	3	0	0	161	52	9
CANADA	3	2	1	0	97	83	7
USA	3	1	2	0	59	99	5
URUGUAY	3	0	3	0	31	114	3

Argentina, Canada and
USA qualify for the Finals.

Uruguay qualify
for the repêchage.

Asian Zone

Japan, who had played in all three previous World Cups, and Hong Kong, with a reputation for playing top-quality sevens rugby, were the favoured teams in the Asian Zone, but two rounds were needed before these teams entered the qualifying competition.

Round A saw Sri Lanka qualify with wins over Thailand (30-15) and Singapore (18-15). Round B was just as close, with Sri Lanka beating the higher-ranked Malaysia, before losing out to a stronger Chinese Taipei team (31-27).

The final qualifying stage was held in Singapore in October 1998. Despite having lost 114-12 to Hong Kong in a previous World Cup qualifier, Chinese Taipei recorded their first victory over the former British colony, 30-12. They were not so fortunate in their next game against an explosive Japanese side, which ran in 20 tries to record the third-highest World Cup score – 134-6.

Well, if New Zealand can have Jonah Lomu....

Demoralised, but still in with a chance of second place in the group, Chinese Taipei faced South Korea in their last match. The Koreans had lost their previous games, 12-40 to Japan and 11-20 to Hong Kong, but put in a commanding performance against Chinese Taipei. They scored 13 tries and won 81-21 to claim the runners-up place and the vital repêchage spot on the number of tries scored.

As expected, Japan won all their matches, ending the tournament with an emphatic 47-7 defeat of heart-broken Hong Kong, who ended up bottom of the table.

ASIAN ZONE TABLES

	P	W	L	D	F	A	Pts
ROUND A							
SRI LANKA	2	2	0	0	48	30	6
THAILAND	2	1	1	0	31	41	4
SINGAPORE	2	0	2	0	26	34	2

Sri Lanka qualify for round B.

	P	W	L	D	F	A	Pts
ROUND B							
CHINESE TAIPEI	2	2	0	0	85	42	6
SRI LANKA	2	1	1	0	66	49	4
MALAYSIA	2	0	2	0	28	88	2

Chinese Taipei qualify for round C.

	P	W	L	D	F	A	Pts
ROUND C							
JAPAN	3	3	0	0	221	25	9
SOUTH KOREA	3	1	2	0	104	81	5
CHINESE TAIPEI	3	1	2	0	57	227	5
HONG KONG	3	1	2	0	39	88	5

Japan qualify for the Finals.

South Korea qualify (on tries scored) for the repêchage.

European Zone

With Wales and France pre-selected, the European zone matches were designed to make sure that the other members of the Five Nations – England, Scotland and Ireland – all qualified. Each entered a different qualifying group in the final round, to be played as a triangular tournament on their own home territory. Before that could happen, 27 nations had to compete for the right to be their opposition.

ROUND A

The process began with 15 teams competing in three zones. Ukraine proved far too good for their group, scoring 177 points in four matches, including a 60-0 victory over Yugoslavia. Despite this loss, and the fact that they failed to turn up for the game against Austria, Yugoslavia still finished second. This group saw the only draw of the entire qualification – 9-9 between Israel and Switzerland.

The second group was topped by Croatia, who beat the more-established rugby nations Norway and Bulgaria, as well as Latvia. The best match was Croatia's 46-31 defeat of Bulgaria, with Croatian fullback Anthony Posa scoring an impressive hat-trick of tries.

It was the smallest nation that pulled off the biggest surprise of the entire qualification. Andorra, a mountain state between Spain and France, won all four matches in zone 3 to earn a qualification spot in round B. This was a major feat because the country has only two rugby clubs, plus an occasional side made up from ski instructors.

ROUND A TABLES

	P	W	L	D	F	A	Pts
ZONE I							
UKRAINE	4	4	0	0	177	21	12
YUGOSLAVIA	4	2	2	0	18	70	8
SWITZERLAND	4	1	2	1	40	50	7
ISRAEL	4	1	2	1	46	73	7
AUSTRIA	4	1	3	0	15	82	6

Ukraine qualify for round B.

ZONE 2

CROATIA	4	4	0	0	192	93	12
LATVIA	4	3	1	0	165	52	10
MOLDOVA	4	2	2	0	53	81	8
NORWAY	4	1	3	0	42	125	6
BULGARIA	4	0	4	0	59	171	4

Croatia qualify for round B.

ZONE 3

ANDORRA	4	4	0	0	139	65	12
SWEDEN	4	3	1	0	191	60	10
HUNGARY	4	2	2	0	50	79	8
LITHUANIA	4	1	3	0	70	157	6
LUXEMBOURG	4	0	4	0	27	116	4

Andorra qualify for round B.

EUROPEAN ZONE – ROUND B

The three nations that qualified from round A went into three pools and took on much stronger opposition than they had faced so far.

The 12 new teams that entered the competition at round B were all members of the Fédération Internationale de Rugby Amateur. FIRA is the second division of European rugby after the Five Nations, and includes Italy and Romania, who had both competed in the three World Cup Finals. These two class teams qualified with considerable ease, both winning all four of their games, as did Spain in pool 3. Italy scored a total of 220 points, including a 102-3 hammering of Denmark in which wing Pierpaolo Rotilla scored a hat-trick of tries in each half. Georgia also qualified for the next stage with three wins, losing only to Italy.

Romania fared even better with impressive 83-13 and 74-13 defeats of Belgium and Poland. They also beat the Netherlands 42-13, who, with victories against Ukraine, Poland and Belgium, finished second. Spain could manage only 158 points in total. Their best win, 62-3 against Andorra, included 10 tries. In what became a battle for supremacy of the Iberian peninsular, Portugal took second place in the pool after a hard-fought decider against Spain, which they lost 22-33.

At the end of round B, six countries – Italy, Romania, Spain, Georgia, the Netherlands and Portugal – moved on to the final European Zone matches. There, they were up against England, Scotland and Ireland, with triangular tournaments held at the end of 1998.

ROUND B TABLES

POOL 1

	P	W	L	D	F	A	Pts
ITALY	4	4	0	0	220	62	12
GEORGIA	4	3	1	0	74	60	10
CROATIA	4	2	2	0	105	90	8
RUSSIA	4	1	3	0	85	92	6
DENMARK	4	0	4	0	26	206	4

Italy and Georgia qualify for round C.

POOL 2

ROMANIA	4	4	0	0	238	46	12
NETHERLANDS	4	3	1	0	106	78	10
UKRAINE	4	2	2	0	97	87	8
POLAND	4	1	3	0	58	91	6
BELGIUM	4	0	4	0	44	180	4

Romania and the Netherlands qualify for round C.

POOL 3

SPAIN	4	4	0	0	158	42	12
PORTUGAL	4	3	1	0	120	60	10
GERMANY	4	2	2	0	102	80	8
CZECH REPUBLIC	4	1	3	0	80	105	6
ANDORRA	4	0	4	0	45	216	4

Spain and Portugal qualify for round C.

Olé!

EUROPEAN ZONE – ROUND C

Ireland, Scotland and England finally entered the competition and were expected to win easily against the six qualifiers from round B, but some nations had other ideas. It was almost too easy for Ireland in their first match, and they scored 10 tries in a 70-0 win over Georgia. Romania then disposed of Georgia 27-23. Ireland scored a further 53 points against Romania in a thrilling and free-flowing game, in which the Romanians helped themselves to 35 points and had Irish nerves jangling at times.

Scotland brushed aside Portugal and Spain, scoring 85 points in each match. In the Spanish match, Scottish wing Kenny Logan became the first Scot to score five tries in a match. He might have had six, but was substituted with two minutes to go and his replacement scored the final try.

In the Portugal-Spain match, Spain's Jose Diaz was sent off after 14 minutes, but Portugal failed to make the most of their extra player. They did score the only two tries of the match, but too many mistakes led to Spain kicking six penalties and a drop goal to achieve a narrow 21-17 victory.

In England's first match, numerous scoring records were broken as the powerful English pack ran up a truly massive 110-0 victory over a brave, but totally out-of-their-depth, Dutch team. Italy swept the Netherlands aside 67-7, and then almost created the biggest shock of the qualification process. For long periods, it looked as if they would beat England. It was not until the 77th minute that England got the decisive score that gave them breathing space and an almost undeserved 23-15 victory.

ROUND C TABLES

	P	W	L	D	F	A	Pts
POOL 1							
IRELAND	2	2	0	0	123	35	6
ROMANIA	2	1	1	0	62	76	4
GEORGIA	2	0	2	0	23	97	2

Ireland and Romania qualify for the Finals.
Georgia qualify for the repêchage.

	P	W	L	D	F	A	Pts
POOL 2							
SCOTLAND	2	2	0	0	170	14	6
SPAIN	2	1	1	0	24	102	4
PORTUGAL	2	0	2	0	28	106	2

Scotland and Spain qualify for the Finals.

Portugal qualify for the repêchage.

	P	W	L	D	F	A	Pts
POOL 3							
ENGLAND	2	2	0	0	133	15	6
ITALY	2	1	1	0	82	30	4
NETHERLANDS	2	0	2	0	7	177	2

England and Italy qualify for the Finals.

Netherlands qualify for the repêchage.

Pacific Zone

The Pacific zone contained the fewest teams, with only seven countries including some of the smallest nations on Earth, such as Tonga, Tahiti, Fiji and the Cook Islands. These all have a great rugby tradition, spurred on by their bigger, more experienced rugby-playing neighbours Australia and New Zealand.

In round A, although Papua New Guinea scored the most points in the group, including a 92-6 hammering of Tahiti, they were beaten into second place by the Cook Islands, 19-22. The Cook Islands went on to play Fiji and Tonga, both of which had featured in previous World Cup Finals and were, unsurprisingly, easily out-pointed by their neighbours. Fiji won 53-7 and Tonga recorded a 68-12 victory. Both went through to round C to face the might of Australia and Western Samoa, with all games played in Australia.

As expected, Australia won all three games, including a difficult 25-13 victory over Western Samoa, to finish top of their group. The Aussies' other games were a good deal easier and they beat Fiji 66-20 and Tonga 74-0. Fiji ended up in second place, beating Tonga 32-15 and Western Samoa 26-18. Having failed to register a win, Tonga were left to compete in the repêchage.

PACIFIC ZONE TABLES

	P	W	L	D	F	A	Pts
ROUND A							
COOK ISLANDS	2	2	0	0	62	19	6
PAPUA NEW GUINEA	2	1	1	0	111	28	4
TAHITI	2	0	2	0	56	132	2

Cook Islands qualify for round B.

	P	W	L	D	F	A	Pts
ROUND B							
FIJI	2	2	0	0	73	17	6
TONGA	2	1	1	0	78	32	4
COOK ISLANDS	2	0	2	0	19	121	2

Fiji and Tonga qualify for round C.

ROUND C

AUSTRALIA	3	3	0	0	165	33	9
FIJI	3	2	1	0	78	99	7
WESTERN SAMOA	3	1	2	0	59	71	5
TONGA	3	0	3	0	35	134	3

Australia, Fiji and Western Samoa qualify for the Finals.

Tonga qualify for the repêchage.

STATS 'N' STUFF

In the Western Samoa v Tonga game, in the 1999 qualifying tournament, Va'aiga Tuigamala from Western Samoa had four cousins playing for the opposition. He still managed to win the Man of the Match award.

By the way, Auntie sends her love.

The Repêchage

In the draw for the final stage of the qualifying process, Morocco were given a bye to the second round. The other six teams had to play home and away ties in the first round.

Tonga comfortably beat Georgia in the first game and were winning the return match 27-15 with only 10 minutes remaining. A late flurry, including two tries, gave the Georgians a narrow 28-27 victory, but the tie was awarded to Tonga on aggregate scores.

In the second tie, the Netherlands scraped a victory over South Korea in the first leg. The tie was all over when South Korea scored four tries in the first 20 minutes of the second leg. They went on to demolish the Dutch 78-14, for an impressive aggregate score of 108-45.

Uruguay eased past Portugal to set up a second-round encounter with Morocco. This was the closest match of the repêchage. In the first game, Uruguay's forwards dominated the match but it took a last-minute try from captain Ormaechea to make the score respectable. The second leg was even closer. Morocco won 21-18, but they lost the tie on aggregate by just 24 points to 36.

In the final tie of the entire qualifying tournament, Tonga established a 32-5 lead over South Korea by half-time in the first leg. The Koreans fought back in the second half but still lost the game. In the second leg, the Tongans were in superb form. They scored 50 unanswered points in the second half and won the match 82-15.

REPECHAGE RESULTS
FIRST ROUND

	First leg	Second leg
Tonga v Georgia	37-6	27-28
Tonga win 64-34		
Netherlands v South Korea	31-30	14-78
South Korea win 108-45		
Uruguay v Portugal	46-9	33-24
Urugay win 79-33		

SECOND ROUND

Morocco v Uruguay	3-18	21-18
Uruguay win 36-24		
Tonga v South Korea	58-26	82-15
Tonga win 140-41		

Uruguay and Tonga qualify for the Finals

THE QUALIFIERS

After 134 qualifying games, the original 66 nations have been whittled down to the final 20 listed below.

COUNTRY	HOW THEY QUALIFIED
Argentina	Winners of American zone
Australia	Winners of Pacific zone
Canada	Second place in American zone
England	Winners of European zone 3
Fiji	Second place in Pacific zone
France	Third place in 1995
Ireland	Winners of European zone 1
Italy	Second place in European zone 3
Japan	Winners of Asian zone
Namibia	Winners of African zone
New Zealand	Runners-up in 1995
Romania	Second place in European zone 1
Scotland	Winners of European zone 2
South Africa	Winners in 1995
Spain	Second place in European zone 2
Tonga	Winners of repêchage 1
Uruguay	Winners of repêchage 2
USA	Third place in American zone
Wales	Hosts
Western Samoa	Third place in Pacific zone

STATS 'N' STUFF

The best individual international scoring performance came in a World Cup qualifier in 1994, when Ashley Billington, the Hong Kong wing, scored 10 tries in a 164-13 win over Singapore.

Argentina

Team colours

Light-blue and white hoops

World Cup record

1987: First round
1991: First round
1995: First round
Played 9, won 1, lost 8
Points for 156; against 260

World ranking

12

KEY PLAYER

Gonzalo Quesada – 25-year-old fly-half who scored 57 points in the two qualifying games against USA and Canada. Very fit, as you would expect from a physical eduction student.

OTHER PLAYERS TO WATCH OUT FOR

Diego Albanese – Wing who played in the 1995 Finals

Frederico Mendez – Hooker who has played for English club sides Bath and Northampton in recent seasons

Pedro Sporledor – Captain and lock who has more than 50 caps. He is more than 2m tall.

State of play

Argentina play an aggressive form of rugby linked to the strength of their forwards. They will hope that this will be sufficient to overcome the opposition, including Wales, who they play in the first match of the entire tournament at the new Millennium Stadium. This match will establish whether Argentina are a force to be reckoned with or are still also-rans.

1999 World Cup chances

They will be engaged in two fiercely competitive games against Wales and Western Samoa, who beat them in the last two World Cups. Their only success will probably be against Japan in their last match. Third place in their pool might just be good enough to qualify for the knock-out stage.

STATS 'N' STUFF

It was on Argentina's 1965 tour of southern Africa that a Rhodesian journalist gave them the nickname of the Pumas, a name that persists, despite the fact that the animal on their badge is a jaguar.

SPOT the difference!

Jaguar   Puma.

Australia

Team colours

Gold and green.

World Cup record

1987: Semi-finalists
1991: Champions
1995: Quarter-finalists
Played 16, won 12, lost 4,
Points for 421; against 229.

World ranking

2

KEY PLAYER

Jason Little – Solid centre with more than 50 caps, he played in the last two World Cup Finals. He scored four tries in the recent qualifying game against Fiji.

OTHER PLAYERS TO WATCH OUT FOR

John Eales – Lock, place-kicker and captain who played in the last two World Cups.

Tim Horan – 29-year-old centre, he played in the 1991 and 1995 Finals.

Joe Roff – All-purpose back who scored three tries in the 1995 Finals, and two in the qualifiers.

State of play

As in most sports, Australia have to be taken seriously. They travel well, as they showed by winning the World Cup in Europe on the only previous occasion it was played there. As one of the three all-conquering southern hemisphere teams they are highly regarded. They have great strength in depth, with many young and largely untried players as well as older, more experienced campaigners. They will hope that with their experience and natural talent they will repeat their achievement of 1991.

1999 World Cup chances

Semi-finalists at the very least. Once there, who knows?

STATS 'N' STUFF

One of the early Australian touring teams, known as the Second Wallabies, returned home undefeated. They arrived in Britain just as the Second World War started and didn't get to play a single match.

Canada

Team colours

Red and white

World Cup record

1987: First round
1991: Quarter-finalists
1995: First round
Played 10, won 3, lost 7
Points for 168; against 202

World ranking

13

KEY PLAYER

John Graf – Scrum-half in the last two World Cup Finals, but he has been capped in four different back positions. Canadian captain, he scored two tries in the qualifying tournament.

OTHER PLAYERS TO WATCH OUT FOR

Joe Pagano – Wing who made his debut in 1997. He has scored three tries in his first seven internationals

Gareth Rees – 32-year-old fly-half and place kicker, and Canada's all-time record points scorer.

Bobby Ross – Full-back who has scored more than 200 points for his country.

State of play

Very physical and sometimes too aggressive, Canada undoubtedly have the skills to beat the also-rans of the world and can give the top teams a good game. Only once have they defeated a 'Top Eight' country, and they need to do this more often to achieve real success. If they can maintain discipline, they should reach the play-offs for the quarter-final stage.

1999 World Cup chances

The three countries they face in the first round will provide strong opposition. They may just get second place in their pool, but are more likely to be third after Fiji and France.

STATS 'N' STUFF

The first ever tour to Canada by a New Zealand XV took place before the First World War. The matches were actually played in California, USA.

England

Team colours

White

World Cup record

1987: Quarter-finalists
1991: Runners-up
1995: Semi-finalists
Played 16, won 10, lost 5
Points for 380; against 255.

World ranking

4

KEY PLAYER

Jeremy Guscott – Multi-talented centre, as he showed with four tries against the Netherlands in qualifying. He can always be relied upon to attempt something different, like kicking a winning drop goal in the dying minutes, as he did for the British Lions against South Africa in 1987.

OTHER PLAYERS TO WATCH OUT FOR

Neil Back – Flanker who scored four tries in the qualifying game against the Netherlands.

Jonny Wilkinson – The new wonder boy of English rugby, he has quickly established himself as the team's goal-kicker as well as a key centre.

State of play

England gave impressive displays against Australia and South Africa at the end of 1998, and they have every chance of doing well in the World Cup, especially as their forwards are strong enough to compete with every other major nation. Unfortunately, England have frequently struggled to perform at their best when expected to win. Recent prime examples include the defeat by Wales in the Five Nations earlier this year and when they almost lost against Italy in the final qualifying match.

1999 World Cup chances

With home advantage for most of the tournament, England should reach the semi-finals, provided they can keep their concentration. From there, anything could happen.

STATS 'N' STUFF

England won the 1881 international against Wales by seven goals, six tries and a drop goal – to nil. If today's scoring system had been in place, the result would have been 82-0, a score that would have stood as a record for England until they defeated the Netherlands 110-0 in 1998.

Fiji

Team colours

White and black

World Cup record

1987: Quarter-finalists
1991: First round
1995: Did not qualify
Played 7, won 1, lost 6
Points for 99, against 195

New Zealand

World ranking

7

KEY PLAYER

Waisale Serevi – Regarded as the best sevens player in the world, Serevi is also a superb place-kicker, scoring 22 points in the qualification victory over Fiji.

OTHER PLAYERS TO WATCH OUT FOR

Fero Lasagavibau – 23-year-old wing, he has scored 13 tries for Fiji.

Nickie Little – Scrum-half and occasional place-kicker, he has scored more than 100 points for his country.

Apisai Naevo – 26-year-old flanker who scores tries, such as the important one against Tonga in the qualifiers.

State of play

The fast, attractive Fijian rugby can unlock any defence, and is ideally suited to the seven-a-side game, which they dominate. They have trouble producing tall, strong players, which means their forward-play and defence is weak. Expect high-scoring games, which could go either way, especially if they are allowed to run at the opposition.

1999 World Cup chances

Despite their obvious flair, Fiji have a tendency to struggle against bigger and more powerful teams, but their attacking play should be good enough to gain them victories over both Canada and Namibia and a place in the play-offs. They could spring a surprise and beat France to go straight into the quarter-finals, but that will probably depend more on the French than the Fijians.

STATS'N'STUFF

The Fijians are current world champions at rugby sevens, having won the Melrose Cup in 1997, defeating South Africa 24-21 in a thrilling final.

France

Team colours

Dark-blue and white

World Cup record

1987: Runners-up
1991: Quarter-finalists
1995: Third
Played 16, won 12, lost 3,
drawn 1
Points for 491, against 244.

World ranking

5

KEY PLAYER

Emile Ntamak – A lightning-fast and tricky 29-year-old full-back, his average is two tries every three games played. Tall and powerful, he is a superb tackler, making him an ideal all-round player.

OTHER PLAYERS TO WATCH OUT FOR

Abdel Benazzi – Flanker of more than 2m tall, he is fast and strong and capable of scoring crucial tries.

Philippe Benetton – 31-year-old flanker who made his international debut in 1989. He is the perfect foil for Benazzi on the opposite side of the scrum.

Christophe Lamaison – Despite being only an occasional kicker, his average is almost 10 points per game at international level.

State of play

Despite being ranked third in the world at the end of 1998, France were in complete disarray for much of the 1999 Five Nations. They recorded their worst sequence of results for many years and their confidence is utterly shattered. Many players seem to be unwilling to play for their country, and divisions within the team are threatening to destroy its chances, even before the Finals start. France have home advantage, but will it be enough?

1999 World Cup chances

Much will depend on whether they can put the disastrous results of early 1999 behind them and regain their spirit. On paper, France should beat all three first-round opponents, but all are capable of springing a surprise. The aggressive nature of the Canadians and Namibians especially will test the resolve of the French, while the Fijians' free-flowing style could exploit any weaknesses within their defence. If there is going to be a surprise result in the tournament, look for it in this group. France may not even make the play-offs.

STATS'N'STUFF

The founder of the modern Olympic Games, Frenchman Baron Pierre de Coubertin, was also organiser and referee of the first French rugby championships in 1892.

Ireland

Team colours

Green and white

World Cup record

1987: Quarter-finalists
1991: Quarter-finalists
1995: Quarter-finalists
Played 12, won 6, lost 6
Points for 324; against 274

World ranking

10

KEY PLAYER

John Bell – 25-year-old centre who scored tries against both Romania and Georgia in qualifying.

OTHER PLAYERS TO WATCH OUT FOR

Eric Elwood – Veteran fly-half and place-kicker, he has scored more than 200 points for Ireland.

Paddy Johns – Dynamic line-out jumper, he played in all five games in the 1995 Finals.

Conor O'Shea – Lively full-back who plays for London Irish and scored tries in both qualifiers.

State of play

Recent successes have depended more on the great team spirit shown by all Irish sides than individual talent. The same is still true, but the draw has once again been kind, with Australia being the only team of any note among their first-round opponents.

1999 World Cup chances

Ireland should finish their pool games second, behind one of the favourites Australia. They will then face the best third-placed team, which they should beat to make a fourth successive quarter-final appearance. They will certainly need the luck of the Irish to progress any further.

STATS 'N' STUFF

In their first international appearance in 1876, Ireland played in green and white hoops, but for the next international, two years later, they were in all-white – the same as their opponents England, which must have been somewhat confusing for all concerned.

Italy

Team colours

Blue and white

World Cup record

1987: First round
1991: First round
1995: First round
Played 9, won 3, lost 6
Points for 133; against 317

World ranking

11

KEY PLAYER

Diego Dominguez – Fly-half and place-kicker, now 33 years old, he has played in all three World Cup Finals. He is in the top 10 of the world's all-time points scorers, having scored more than 600 international points in a glittering career.

OTHER PLAYERS TO WATCH OUT FOR

Carlo Checchinato – Number 8, he scored twice against the Netherlands in qualifying.

Marcello Cuttitta – Wing who has played in all three World Cup Finals, scoring more than 100 points for his country.

Massimo Cuttitta – Twin of Marcello, but weighs 20kg more than his brother. He played at prop in the 1991 and 1995 Finals.

State of play

Italy has a strong and solid pack and a well-organised defence. In 2000, they will join Europe's rugby elite in the 'Six' Nations Championships, but their overall play is still not as good as that of the top nations. They lack the killer touch to pull off an upset, as England found to their good fortune in qualifying. That narrow defeat may give the Italians the confidence they need to take on and beat higher-ranked opponents and progress beyond the group stages for the first time.

1999 World Cup chances

They should finish third in their group, but their results may not be good enough to earn them the vital best third-place spot and a place in the play-offs. It may all come down to tries scored, or even players sent off.

STATS 'N' STUFF

Italian club rugby has attracted many foreign celebrities, many of them of Italian descent. The most famous is the Australian wing David Campese, who played for Milan.

Japan

Team colours

Red and white

World Cup record

1987: First round
1991: First round
1995: First round
Played 9, won 1, lost 8
Points for 180; against: 462

World ranking

18

KEY PLAYER

Keiji Hirose – 26-year-old fly-half who scored 64 points with his boot in two qualifying matches, plus a try against Hong Kong. His only World Cup Finals appearance so far was in the record defeat by New Zealand (17-145).

OTHER PLAYERS TO WATCH OUT FOR

Andrew McCormick – New Zealand-born centre and captain.

Osami Masuho – Wing, who scored five tries in the huge win over Chinese Taipei (134-6).

Ko Nakumura – Flanker who scored a try against Ireland in the 1995 World Cup Finals.

State of play

Japanese players are fast across the ground and ferocious in the tackle. They tend to be small in stature and therefore unable to compete in key areas such as the line-out and scrum, which often leads to a lack of possession. They have proved that they can score tries, and they will hope that their speed makes up for their lack of strength. It just depends on whether they can protect their own line as well.

1999 World Cup chances

Japan easily qualified with record-breaking performances. They are ranked in the top 20 but will probably not win a game, although defeats of the magnitude of the record 145-13 drubbing by New Zealand in 1995 are unlikely to be repeated.

STATS 'N' STUFF

One early Japanese translation for rugby was 'the fighting game'. Despite this, violence in club rugby today is virtually unknown.

Namibia

Team colours

Blue, red and white

World Cup record

First appearance in the Finals

World ranking

21

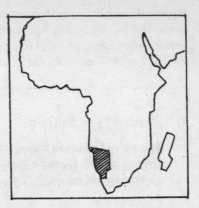

KEY PLAYER

Lean Van Dyk – 23-year-old full-back who scored a vital 14 points in the tightly contested qualifying match against Zimbabwe, including one try and three conversions.

OTHER PLAYERS TO WATCH OUT FOR

Quinn Hough – Number 8 with an impressive try record, including two against Ivory Coast.

Attie Samuelson – Wing who scored tries in both qualifiers against Ivory Coast and Zimbabwe.

Johan Zaayman – Fly-half who scored Namibia's only try against Morocco in the final qualifier.

State of play

Namibia play an aggressive, fast moving style of rugby, similar in many ways to that of their neighbour South Africa. They did well to qualify as African zone winners because they had to go through two sets of qualifying matches. On the way, they avenged a previous World Cup qualifying defeat by Ivory Coast and beat Zimbabwe and Morocco. Their stubborn resistance may surprise a few people and they will be hoping that their style will unsettle their first-round opponents, France, Canada and Fiji.

1999 World Cup chances

Expect three hard-fought games, but no upsets. They have achieved a great deal just by qualifying, and last place in their group is the best they can hope for.

STATS ' N ' STUFF

Namibia were not eligible for inclusion in the first World Cup in 1987, because the country did not officially exist until 1990, when it gained its independence from South Africa.

New Zealand

Team colours

Black

World Cup record

1987: Champions
1991: Third
1995: Runners-up
Played 18, won 15, lost 3
Points for 778; against 235

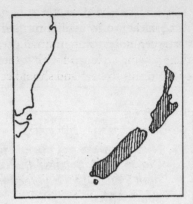

World ranking

3

KEY PLAYER

Christian Cullen – 23-year-old full-back rated as the best attacking player in the world. He has scored 21 tries in his first 22 matches. Fast and powerful, his tackling makes him an effective last line of defence.

OTHER PLAYERS TO WATCH OUT FOR

Todd Blackadder – All-round forward and hard-hitting tackler.

Jonah Lomu – Monster 1.96m wing who is built more like a forward. He destroyed England in 1995 with four tries.

Carlos Spencer – 23-year-old fly-half who has already scored more than 250 points for New Zealand.

State of play

Having won the first World Cup, the All Blacks have, by their own high standards, failed in the last two competitions, although they reached the final four years ago. Still recognised as one of the best rugby-playing nations in the world, they expect to win, not just every game they compete in, but the tournament itself.

1999 World Cup chances

The All Blacks are not the team of old and have slipped to number three in the world behind rivals Australia and South Africa. They are currently undergoing internal personnel changes that have affected their playing style, and with it their success rate. They will still be one of the teams to beat and should easily make the quarter-finals.

STATS 'N' STUFF

In 1888-89, New Zealand were the first overseas team to tour Great Britain and they played a record number of games. They also performed the haka - the Maori war dance – before each game. It was the first time this had been seen in the British Isles and perhaps it contributed to the New Zealanders' number of victories.

Romania

Team colours

Yellow, red and blue.

World Cup record

1987: First round
1991: First round
1995: First round
Played 9, won 2, lost 7
Points for 106; against 291.

World ranking

17

KEY PLAYER

Petre Mitu – Scrum-half and place-kicker, and all-time top scorer for Romania. He contributed a try, three conversions and two penalties to the vital qualification win over Georgia.

OTHER PLAYERS TO WATCH OUT FOR

Gabriel Brezoianu – Centre who scored tries in both qualifiers in Ireland.

Gheorghe Solomie – Experienced wing, he scored a try against Ireland

Mihai Vioreanu – Attacking full-back, he scored two tries against Ireland and one against Georgia.

State of play

A strong pack, fast running backs and a game based around the principles of the free-flowing French points to the strong possibility that Romania will be giant-killers. On their day, they are capable of beating many of the top teams, but they lack consistency and a belief in themselves. Although they beat Scotland in 1984 and 1991, and Wales in 1983 and 1988, they have never really fulfilled their promise. They have competed in all three World Cups and notched up two wins – against Zimbabwe in 1987 and Fiji in 1991 – but they have been overtaken by Italy as the sixth force in European rugby.

1999 World Cup chances

They should be soundly beaten in their first game against Australia and will need to pick themselves up after that, because their next match, against USA, will be vital. A good result could put them on track for a shock result against Ireland. The best they can really hope for is third place in the pool and another crack at the Irish in the play-offs.

STATS 'N' STUFF

A Romanian rugby team competed in the 1924 Olympics. They were soundly beaten by both France and the USA but still won the bronze medal because only three teams took part.

Scotland

Team colours

Dark-blue and white.

World Cup record

1987: Quarter-finalists
1991: Semi-finalists
1995: Quarter-finalists
Played 14, won 8, lost 5, drawn 1
Points for 479; against 237

World ranking

6

KEY PLAYER

Kenny Logan – Record-breaking speedster on the wing, he scored five tries against Spain and another two against Portugal in qualifying games. He has also established himself as Scotland's most reliable place-kicker since Gavin Hastings.

OTHER PLAYERS TO WATCH OUT FOR

Rowen Shepherd – Full-back and place-kicker, he is only the sixth Scottish player to score more than 100 points for his country.

Gregor Townsend – Tricky and elusive fly-half-cum-centre who has played club rugby in Scotland, England and France.

George 'Dodie' Weir – One of the tallest men in the Finals, at more than 2m, he uses his height to great effect in line-outs.

State of play

In recent years, Scotland lost a number of key players, which left them struggling against virtually every international team they played. After some embarrassingly heavy defeats at the hands of the southern hemisphere teams, they then inflicted their own crushing defeats of both Portugal and Spain in the qualifying games. They won the 1999 Five Nations tournament, showing that they have put the bad spell behind them. They will be expecting to defeat all but the very best teams in the World Cup.

1999 World Cup chances

Scotland will play all their early matches in the friendly and noisy confines of their home ground, Murrayfield, in Edinburgh, which should work to their advantage. Working against them is the fact that they will face world champions, South Africa, in their opening match. After that, they will have an easy ride and should easily progress to the quarter-finals.

STATS 'N' STUFF

Scotland boast the oldest rugby club in the world –
Edinburgh Academicals, which was founded in 1858,
four years before Blackheath, the oldest English club.

South Africa

Team colours

Olive green with gold trim

World Cup record

1987: Did not enter
1991: Did not enter
1995: Champions
Played 6, won 6, lost 0
Points for 144; against 67

World ranking

1

KEY PLAYER

Joost van der Westhuizen – Regarded as the best scrum-half in the world, partly due to his performances in the last World Cup. In the final, his fierce tackling of players such as Jonah Lomu restricted the New Zealanders' scoring chances and set up a famous win.

OTHER PLAYERS TO WATCH OUT FOR

Henry Honiball – Fly-half nicknamed 'Blade' because of his ability to slice through opposition defences.

Percy Montgomery – 25-year-old who can play at full-back, centre or on the wing and score tries from all positions.

Pieter Rossouw – Tall wing with outstanding pace and handling.

State of play

Following the abolition of the country's apartheid regime in 1900, South Africa's international sporting ban was lifted after almost 30 years, and it was chosen to be the host of the 1995 World Cup. That the team could compete at the top level after so many years in the wilderness was amazing. That it actually won, was nothing short of miraculous. As reigning world champions, and with the vast majority of the team that won four years ago still playing, South Africa are fancied to do well again.

1999 World Cup chances

South Africa are many experts' pre-tournament favourites, and it will take a mighty performance to pull the trophy from their grasp. They should definitely be finalists, and probably winners.

STATS'N'STUFF

Shipping tycoon Donald Currie gave a cup to one of the first British Lions touring teams to donate to South African rugby. This became the Currie Cup, for which South African provincial sides still compete.

Spain

Team colours

Red and yellow

World Cup record

First appearance in
the Finals

World ranking

22

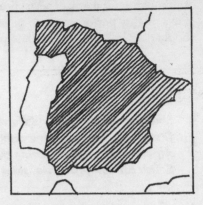

KEY PLAYER

Andrei Kovalenco – 28-year-old fly-half and place-kicker, he
effectively ensured Spain's inclusion in the Finals with six penalties in
the all-important deciding qualifier against Portugal.

OTHER PLAYERS TO WATCH OUT FOR

Asier Altuna – Prop with more than 30 caps, including appearances
in the last two World Cup Finals.

Rafael Bastide – Able to play at wing or full-back, he scored two tries
in four qualifying games.

Alberto Malo – With more than 60 caps as flanker, many as captain,
he is the most experienced player in the Spanish side.

State of play

The closest Spain ever came to true international recognition, prior
to this year's World Cup, was in 1991 when they finished third in the
European qualifying group behind Italy and Romania, just missing
out on a trip to the Finals. This time, they made sure of their place
when they beat Portugal at Murrayfield.

1999 World Cup chances

They must hope that all their opponents have an off-day. Not only
will they have to face hard-hitting Uruguay, but their next match will
be against reigning champions South Africa. They will then come up

against Scotland who will be on their home turf. In the qualifiers, Scotland beat Spain 85-3, so Spain will probably finish bottom of their pool.

STATS 'N' STUFF

In 1931 and 1932 Spain played just four 'internationals' – all against the French Foreign Legion. They won one, lost two and drew one. Scoring was low, with a combined total of 52-34 in favour of the French.

Tonga

Team colours

Scarlet and white

World Cup record

1987: First round
1991: Did not qualify
1995: First round
Played 6, won 1, lost 5
Points for 73; against 188

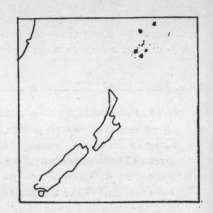

World ranking

14

KEY PLAYER

Brian Wooley – 22-year-old fly-half who plays club rugby in New Zealand. He is a great all-rounder and is occasionally the place-kicker.

OTHER PLAYERS TO WATCH OUT FOR

Pierre Hola – Powerful running full-back and accurate place-kicker.

Matt Te Pou Jr. – Try-scoring flanker who plays club rugby in New Zealand.

Fe'ao Vunipola – Hooker and captain, who played in the 1995 World Cup Finals.

State of play

The Tongans like playing fast-running rugby, but they also have a reputation for hard-hitting, no-nonsense defence. That will need to be at its very best in all three games in the first round, but they could be one of the teams to cause an upset in the tournament. They have an almost impossible start against arch rivals New Zealand, but then a relatively easy game against Italy. A good result against them could set up a classic encounter against England.

1999 World Cup chances

They should finish third in their group and if their defence can hold out, especially against New Zealand, they may get through to the play-off stage as best third-placed team.

STATS 'N' STUFF

Some of the native-born Tongans play for other countries, for example, Jonah Lomu plays for New Zealand and Willie Ofahengaue plays for Australia. At the next World Cup in 2003, these players will have to play for their country of birth, which could mean an upsurge in Tongan rugby success.

United States of America

Team colours

Red, white and blue.

World Cup record

1987: First round
1991: First round
1995: First round
Played 6, won 1, lost 5
Points for 63; against 212

World ranking

16

KEY PLAYER

Vaea Anitoni – Wing who is the most-experienced US player with more than 30 caps and, more importantly, more than 100 international points to his credit.

OTHER PLAYERS TO WATCH OUT FOR

Tom Billups – Hooker and captain, with more than 30 caps.

Alatini Saulala – 31-year-old centre whose average is one try every two games.

Mark Williams – Number 8, he played in the last two World Cups, scoring 16 points a game as a place-kicker.

State of play

As befits the most powerful nation on earth, the USA have a strong and impressive line-up of players, but they are short on international experience. Against teams such as Spain, Namibia and Japan this would not create a problem, but their group matches are against Ireland, Australia and Romania, all of whom are strong, powerful and far more experienced. The USA's only hope is that their opponents have a bad day.

1999 World Cup chances

The USA should put up fierce resistance, but they are unlikely to trouble the scorekeepers too greatly. This is a pity, because the failure of the 'Eagles' will set the sport back a long way in their country, which likes to win at all costs.

STATS 'N' STUFF

The United States are the reigning Olympic champions. They won the gold medal in 1924, when rugby was last played at the Games, and in 1920.

Uruguay

Team colours

Sky-blue

World Cup record

First appearance in the Finals

World ranking

19

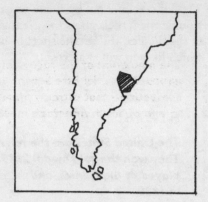

KEY PLAYER

Pablo Lemoine – 24-year-old try-scoring prop, whose hard-hitting style makes him an inspirational leader in the pack. He scored two tries and was Man of the Match in the first repêchage game against Portugal. He has played in the English league for Bristol.

OTHER PLAYERS TO WATCH OUT FOR

Diego Ormaechea – Number 8 and captain who won his first cap 20 years ago. At 40, he will be the oldest player in the tournament.

Federico Sciarro – Scrum-half and place-kicker, he is Uruguay's top points scorer in their short rugby-union history. It was perhaps due to his kicking that Uruguay achieved their place in these Finals.

Diego Aguirre – 25-year-old fly-half and excellent ball-handler, he is only just beginning to show what a fine player he is.

State of play

Although they have a strong pack that dominated weaker teams, such as Portugal, in the qualification process, Uruguay could quite easily be cannon-fodder for South Africa and Scotland, who will be looking to amass some points.

1999 World Cup chances

Will probably find World Cup glory in their game against Spain, but will not progress beyond Pool stage.

STATS ' N ' STUFF

The high point of the rugby calendar in Uruguay is the annual Punte del Este Sevens, an international competition that attracts players from all over the world to one of South America's most luxurious beach resorts.

Wales

Team colours

Red

World Cup record

1987: Third
1991: First round
1995: First round
Played 11, won 6, lost 5
Points for 225; against 212

World ranking

9

KEY PLAYER

Neil Jenkins – With more than 600 international points to his name, he is regarded as one of the great all-time place-kickers. He is equally at home as full-back or fly-half, making him a superb team player.

OTHER PLAYERS TO WATCH OUT FOR

Robert Howley – Strong and powerful scrum-half who will celebrate his 29th birthday on the day before the Wales-Western Samoa match.

Scott Quinnell – Strong Number 8 known for his hard, punishing tackles.

Arwyl Thomas – Small fly-half with a terrific turn of foot and brilliant ball-handling skills.

State of play

Wales will be hoping for much better performances than they gave in the last two World Cup competitions. Their first match will be against the impressive Argentines and they will then have to face the Western Samoans, who beat them in 1991, and Japan. These matches will be far from easy but the experience of the Welsh and the confidence they have gained from beating England earlier this year, should see them through.

1999 World Cup chances

Two wins will be enough to see Wales into the play-offs, but they should make their home advantage count and win all three matches in the first round and progress directly to the quarter-finals. This may be as far as they get.

STATS 'N' STUFF

After Wales narrowly beat Western Samoa in 1989, Welsh player Gareth Davies suggested that it was a good thing that they hadn't been playing the whole of Samoa because they might have lost. Two years later, his fears were realised. The Western Samoans beat the Welsh in the 1991 World Cup – without any help – and Wales failed to qualify for the next stage.

Western Samoa

Team colours

Royal-blue and white.

World Cup record

1987: Did not appear
1991: Quarter-finalists
1995: Quarter-finalists
Played 8, won 4, lost 4
Points for 192; against 170

World ranking

8

KEY PLAYER

Va'aiga Tuigamala – Hard-hitting and hard-running centre who was a world champion at rugby league with the English club Wigan before he changed to the union code, with English club Newcastle. He was an inspirational Man of the Match in the important qualifier against Tonga.

OTHER PLAYERS TO WATCH OUT FOR

Pat Lam – Explosive flanker who played in the last two World Cup Finals

Brian Lima – Fast and effective wing who has scored more than 50 international points in his career.

Junior Paramore – Flanker currently playing club rugby in England.

State of play

With hard-hitting forwards and fast, elusive backs, the Western Samoans play an even more aggressive game than their neighbours, the All Blacks. They will be hoping that this will be enough to earn them another famous victory against Wales and, in the third successive World Cup, against Argentina.

1999 World Cup chances

They should beat Japan and Argentina to secure a play-off place at the very least. Their match against Wales will probably be the group decider, and the Welsh will not relish taking on the fired-up Samoans again on their home turf.

STATS 'N' STUFF

The first international that Western Samoa played was against Fiji in 1924. There was an interesting obstacle – a large tree virtually in the middle of the pitch.

PREVIOUS WORLD CUPS
1987 – Australia and New Zealand

Sixteen nations were invited to take part in the first ever rugby union World Cup without any pre-qualifying. It was fitting that the best team, New Zealand, should carry all before them to reach the Final. Some of their early opposition was not of the highest quality, but the Kiwis did dispose of Scotland and Wales in the knock-out stages with a combined score of 79-9. The first close game was between Scotland and France in their opening pool match, which ended in a nail-biting 20-20 draw. That match is still the only game in World Cup Finals history to end in a draw. France finished top of their group and progressed to the semi-finals, where they played a match against Australia that is regarded as a true classic. This epic encounter saw the lead change hands a number of times until France clinched the match in the final seconds with a dazzling and quite spectacular try by full-back Serge Blanco.

The final was set for a north-south confrontation, but it really was no contest. New Zealand overpowered the French 29-9 to win the William Webb Ellis Trophy in front of a packed home crowd at Eden Park, Auckland. Two tries in two minutes in the second half sealed a superb victory, and four penalties, a conversion and a drop goal from the boot of Grant Fox established him as the highest points scorer.

Results and tables

POOL ONE

AUSTRALIA	19	ENGLAND	6
USA	21	JAPAN	18
ENGLAND	60	JAPAN	7
AUSTRALIA	47	USA	12
ENGLAND	34	USA	6
AUSTRALIA	42	JAPAN	24

	P	W	L	D	F	A	Pts
AUSTRALIA	3	3	0	0	108	41	6
ENGLAND	3	2	1	0	100	32	4
USA	3	1	2	0	39	99	2
JAPAN	3	0	3	0	48	123	0

POOL TWO

CANADA	37	TONGA	4
WALES	13	IRELAND	6
WALES	29	TONGA	16
IRELAND	46	CANADA	19
WALES	40	CANADA	9
IRELAND	32	TONGA	9

	P	W	L	D	F	A	Pts
WALES	3	3	0	0	82	31	6
IRELAND	3	2	1	0	84	41	4
CANADA	3	1	2	0	65	90	2
TONGA	3	0	3	0	29	98	0

POOL THREE

N. ZEALAND	70	ITALY	6
FIJI	28	ARGENTINA	9
N. ZEALAND	74	FIJI	13
ARGENTINA	25	ITALY	16
ITALY	18	FIJI	15
N. ZEALAND	46	ARGENTINA	15

	P	W	L	D	F	A	Pts
NEW ZEALAND	3	3	0	0	190	34	6
FIJI	3	2	1	0	56	101	4
ARGENTINA	3	1	2	0	49	90	2
ITALY	3	0	3	0	40	110	0

POOL FOUR

ROMANIA	21	ZIMBABWE	20
FRANCE	20	SCOTLAND	20
FRANCE	55	ROMANIA	12
SCOTLAND	60	ZIMBABWE	21
FRANCE	70	ZIMBABWE	12
SCOTLAND	55	ROMANIA	28

	P	W	L	D	F	A	Pts
FRANCE	3	2	0	1	145	44	5
SCOTLAND	3	2	0	1	135	69	5
ROMANIA	3	1	2	0	61	130	2
ZIMBABWE	3	0	3	0	53	151	0

QUARTER-FINALS

N. ZEALAND	30	SCOTLAND	3
FRANCE	31	FIJI	16
AUSTRALIA	33	IRELAND	15
WALES	16	ENGLAND	3

SEMI-FINALS

| FRANCE | 30 | AUSTRALIA | 24 |
| N. ZEALAND | 49 | WALES | 6 |

THIRD PLACE PLAY-OFF

| WALES | 22 | AUSTRALIA | 21 |

FINAL

N. ZEALAND	29		FRANCE	9
Tries	Kirwan, Gallagher		Blanco	
Conversions	Fox (2)		Cambarebaro	
Penalties	Fox (4)		Cambarebaro	
Drop goals	–		–	

Team performances

Highest score in one match	74 by New Zealand (v Fiji)
Highest total score	74-13 New Zealand v Fiji
Largest margin of victory	70-6 New Zealand v Italy
Most tries in one match	13 by France (v Zimbabwe)

Player performances

Top points scorer	126 by Grant Fox (New Zealand)
Most tries	6 by John Kirwan and Craig Green (both New Zealand)
Most penalties	21 by Grant Fox (New Zealand)
Most drop goals	3 by Jonathan Davies (Wales)
Most points in one match	30 by Didier Cambarebaro (France v Zimbabwe)
Most tries in one match	3 by Iuean Evans (Wales v Canada), Craig Green (New Zealand v Fiji), and John Gallaher (New Zealand v Fiji)
Most penalties in one match	6 by Grant Fox (New Zealand v Argentina and v Scotland)

1991 - England, Scotland, Wales, Ireland and France

After a series of pre-qualifying matches, 16 teams made it through to the second World Cup Finals. As the official host nation, England staged the final at Twickenham.

Western Samoa, who had not received an invitation four years earlier, had a point to prove and did so in great style in their first match by beating Wales in Cardiff. England lost their first match, against world champions New Zealand, but dominated the other pool games, and went on to record famous victories against France in Paris and Scotland in Edinburgh to reach the final. Australia won all three of their pool games and came up against the unfancied Irish in a Dublin quarter-final. The men in green were not such an easy touch. With fly-half Ralph Keyes in fine kicking form, the home side was ahead 18-15 with only seconds remaining. It took a magical try from fly-half Michael Lynagh to snatch a 19-18 victory for Australia. New Zealand struggled against lesser teams such as Canada and Italy, so it was no real surprise when they were beaten 16-6 in the semi-final by Australia.

The final was between Australia and their English hosts, whose over-powering forwards and home advantage made them slight favourites. England abandoned their close-control game in favour of a more open running approach and, despite outplaying Australia for much of the match, lost an uninspired and low-scoring contest 6-12.

Results and tables

POOL ONE

N. ZEALAND	18	ENGLAND	12
ITALY	30	USA	9
N. ZEALAND	46	USA	6
ENGLAND	36	ITALY	6
ENGLAND	37	USA	9
N. ZEALAND	31	ITALY	21

	P	W	L	D	F	A	Pts
N. ZEALAND	3	3	0	0	95	39	6
ENGLAND	3	2	1	0	85	33	4
ITALY	3	1	2	0	57	76	2
USA	3	0	3	0	24	113	0

POOL TWO

SCOTLAND	47	JAPAN	9
IRELAND	55	ZIMBABWE	11
IRELAND	32	JAPAN	16
SCOTLAND	51	ZIMBABWE	12
SCOTLAND	24	IRELAND	15
JAPAN	52	ZIMBABWE	8

	P	W	L	D	F	A	Pts
SCOTLAND	3	3	0	0	122	36	6
IRELAND	3	2	1	0	102	51	4
JAPAN	3	1	2	0	77	87	2
ZIMBABWE	3	0	3	0	31	158	0

POOL THREE

AUSTRALIA	32	ARGENTINA	19
W. SAMOA	16	WALES	13
AUSTRALIA	9	W. SAMOA	3
WALES	16	ARGENTINA	7
AUSTRALIA	38	WALES	3
W. SAMOA	35	ARGENTINA	12

	P	W	L	D	F	A	Pts
AUSTRALIA	3	3	0	0	190	34	6
W. SAMOA	3	2	1	0	56	101	4
WALES	3	1	2	0	49	90	2
ARGENTINA	3	0	3	0	40	110	0

POOL FOUR

FRANCE	30	ROMANIA	3
CANADA	13	FIJI	3
FRANCE	33	FIJI	9
CANADA	19	ROMANIA	11
ROMANIA	17	FIJI	15
FRANCE	19	CANADA	13

	P	W	L	D	F	A	Pts
FRANCE	3	3	0	0	82	25	6
CANADA	3	2	1	0	45	33	4
ROMANIA	3	1	2	0	31	64	2
FIJI	3	0	3	0	27	63	0

QUARTER-FINALS

ENGLAND	19	FRANCE	10
SCOTLAND	28	W. SAMOA	6
AUSTRALIA	19	IRELAND	18
N. ZEALAND	29	CANADA	13

SEMI-FINALS

ENGLAND	9	SCOTLAND	6
AUSTRALIA	16	N. ZEALAND	6

THIRD PLACE PLAY-OFF

N. ZEALAND	13	SCOTLAND	6

FINAL

AUSTRALIA	12	ENGLAND	6
Tries	Daly	–	
Conversions	Lynagh	–	
Penalties	Lynagh (2)	Webb (2)	
Drop goals	–	–	

Team performances

Highest score in one match	55 by Ireland (v Zimbabwe)
Highest total score	55-11 Ireland v Zimbabwe
Largest margin of victory	55-11 Ireland v Zimbabwe
	52-8 Japan v Zimbabwe
Most tries in one match	9 by Japan (v Zimbabwe)

Player performances

Top points scorer	68 by Ralph Keyes (Ireland)
Most tries	6 by David Campese (Australia) and Jean-Baptiste Lafond (France)
Most penalties	16 by Ralph Keyes (Ireland)
Most drop goals	2 by Gareth Rees (Canada), Ralph Keyes (Ireland), Rob Andrew (England) and Rabaka (Fiji)
Most points in one match	23 by Ralph Keyes (Ireland v Zimbabwe)
Most tries in one match	4 by Brian Robinson (Ireland v Zimbabwe)
Most penalties in one match	5 by Ralph Keyes (Ireland v Zimbabwe)

1995 – South Africa

Banned from international sport until 1990, when the country's apartheid regime was abolished, South Africa was chosen to stage the third rugby World Cup. It provided massive stadiums, massive support by rugby-crazy crowds and a massive team capable of competing at the highest level.

Sixteen teams, from an original 43, qualified to take part. There were few shocks with all the major teams except Wales reaching the quarter-finals. One of the most amazing matches took place between New Zealand and Japan. New Zealand fielded many reserve players and still thrashed Japan 145-17 – a world record score.

South Africa, New Zealand, France and England went through to the semi-finals, with England revenging their defeat by Australia in 1991, by beating them this time in the quarter-finals. England faced New Zealand in the semi-finals and could not cope with the devastating power and pace of the new rugby sensation, Jonah Lomu. The massive New Zealand wing tore the English defence to shreds, setting up a well-deserved 45-29 victory. The other semi-final was played in a mud bath, which at times made the game look more like water polo, but South Africa overcame typical French resistance to win 19-15.

82

In the final, South Africa stopped Lomu and New Zealand's running game, and the match became a long hard slog. With the scores level at 9-9 at full time, the match went to extra time. In the end, it was a drop goal from South African Joel Stransky that won the match in the dying moments.

Results and tables

POOL ONE

SOUTH AFRICA	27	AUSTRALIA	18
CANADA	34	ROMANIA	3
SOUTH AFRICA	21	ROMANIA	8
AUSTRALIA	27	CANADA	11
AUSTRALIA	42	ROMANIA	3
SOUTH AFRICA	20	CANADA	0

	P	W	L	D	F	A	Pts
SOUTH AFRICA	3	3	0	0	68	26	6
AUSTRALIA	3	2	1	0	87	41	4
CANADA	3	1	2	0	45	50	2
ROMANIA	3	0	3	0	14	97	0

POOL TWO

W. SAMOA	42	ITALY	18
ENGLAND	24	ARGENTINA	18
W. SAMOA	32	ARGENTINA	26
ENGLAND	27	ITALY	20
ITALY	31	ARGENTINA	25
ENGLAND	44	W. SAMOA	22

	P	W	L	D	F	A	Pts
ENGLAND	3	3	0	0	95	60	6
W. SAMOA	3	2	1	0	96	88	4
ITALY	3	1	2	0	69	94	2
ARGENTINA	3	0	3	0	87	87	0

POOL THREE

WALES	57	JAPAN	10
N. ZEALAND	43	IRELAND	19
IRELAND	50	JAPAN	28
NEW ZEALAND	34	WALES	9
NEW ZEALAND	145	JAPAN	17
IRELAND	24	WALES	23

	P	W	L	D	F	A	Pts
NEW ZEALAND	3	3	0	0	222	45	6
IRELAND	3	2	1	0	93	94	4
WALES	3	1	2	0	89	68	2
JAPAN	3	0	3	0	55	252	0

POOL FOUR

SCOTLAND	89	IVORY COAST	0
FRANCE	38	TONGA	10
FRANCE	54	IVORY COAST	18
SCOTLAND	41	TONGA	5
TONGA	29	IVORY COAST	11
FRANCE	22	SCOTLAND	19

	P	W	L	D	F	A	Pts
FRANCE	3	3	0	0	114	47	6
SCOTLAND	3	2	1	0	149	27	4
TONGA	3	1	2	0	44	90	2
IVORY COAST	3	0	3	0	29	172	0

QUARTER-FINALS

FRANCE	36	IRELAND	12
SOUTH AFRICA	42	W. SAMOA	14
ENGLAND	25	AUSTRALIA	22
NEW ZEALAND	48	SCOTLAND	30

SEMI-FINALS

SOUTH AFRICA	19	FRANCE	15
NEW ZEALAND	45	ENGLAND	29

THIRD PLACE PLAY-OFF

FRANCE	19	ENGLAND	9

FINAL

SOUTH AFRICA	15	N. ZEALAND	12
Tries	–	–	
Conversions	–	–	
Penalties	Stransky (3)	Mehrtens (3)	
Drop goals	Stransky (2)	Mehrtens	

Team performances

Highest score in one match	145 by New Zealand (v Japan)
Highest total score	145-17 New Zealand v Japan
Largest margin of victory	145-17 New Zealand v Japan
Most tries in one match	9 by New Zealand (v Japan)

Player performances

Top points scorer	112 by Thierry Lacroix (France)
Most tries	7 by Marc Ellis and Jonah Lomu (both New Zealand)
Most penalties	26 by Thierry Lacroix (France)
Most drop goals	3 by Andrew Mehrtens (New Zealand), Joel Stransky (South Africa) and Rob Andrew (England)
Most points in one match	45 by Simon Culhane (New Zealand v Japan)
Most tries in one match	6 by Marc Ellis (New Zealand v Japan)
Most penalties in one match	9 by Gavin Hastings (Scotland v Ivory Coast)

PAST WORLD CUP MASTERS

SERGE BLANCO
France

Venezuelan-born Serge Blanco was one of the most entertaining rugby players ever. Originally a fast wing, he became the most-feared counter-attacking full-back of his generation, perhaps of all-time. He was capable of turning rugged defensive play into instant and productive assaults on the opposition's try-line within seconds.

He had a style and a long-legged grace rarely matched in the harsh and sometimes brutal world of international rugby, but his laid-back attitude sometimes got him into trouble. In the final minute of the superb World Cup semi-final between France and Australia in 1987, the scores were tied at 24-24. Blanco then finished off a classic and seemingly endless move that combined back row, centres and wings to score the all-important try that took France to the World Cup final.

Adieu, ma cherie!

In 1995, at Parc de Prince in Paris, France was defeated by Will Carling's rampant England, a match that saw Blanco, then the French captain, pull on his cherished blue jersey for the last time. It was not a fitting end to his glittering career, which included 96 caps and 38 international tries – still a record for his country.

DAVID CAMPESE
Australia

The word 'genius' has often been used to describe Australian David Campese, but when players of the calibre of England centre Jeremy Guscott say 'Campese tries things – that's part of his genius' you need to take notice. One of only a handful of players to have performed in all three World Cup Finals, 'Campo' had the ability to side-step opponents while travelling at full speed. He had pace and power, but his greatest asset was his unpredictability. He was able to see an opening, seize a half-chance and turn it into points on the scoreboard.

Jeremy Guscott knew this, as did all his opponents, but few could do anything about it. Like all the greats in any sport, Campese had the ability to think the unthinkable, do the undoable and frequently score from seemingly impossible positions. Campese also out-thought his opponents off the field. Many experts believe that remarks he made before the 1991 final, about England's lack of running ability, made the English abandon their dominating forward-play tactics, which eventually led to their downfall.

In a Test career that lasted a record 16 years, he acquired 101 caps – the second-largest haul for any player (only Philippe Sella of France has more) – and scored 63 tries.

WILL CARLING
England

A strong-tackling, hard-running centre, Will Carling made his name in world rugby by becoming the most successful English captain ever. Given the task in 1988, at the tender age of 22, Carling always led his troops from the front with an uncompromising style that brought England a succession of Triple Crowns, Five Nations' Grand Slams and an appearance in one World Cup final.

In the all-important World Cup semi-final against France in 1991, Carling scored England's vital try in the dying moments of the game. Launching a high kick at the French defence, he chased it down, tackled the opposition captain, Serge Blanco, and collected the fumble to score the five points that gave England a magnificent 19-10 victory.

Will Carling captained England in two World Cups, displaying all the commitment and solidity that was the hallmark of his game throughout his career. His leadership qualities were perhaps better than his playing abilities, but he forged a fearsome centre partnership with the flamboyant Jeremy Guscott for the majority of his England career. He won 72 caps, 59 of them as captain, and scored 12 international tries, putting him fifth in the all-time try-scoring list of English players.

IEUAN EVANS
Wales

With 71 caps and 32 tries, Ieuan Evans is Wales's most-capped player and top try scorer, as well as being its longest-serving captain (1991-95). He could have achieved even more, but for a number of serious injuries to his shoulder and ankle, which kept him out of the game for many months at a time.

A solid and reliable defender with electrifying pace and the ability to evade tackles, his rise to the top of the game unfortunately coincided with the decline of the Welsh national team. Ieuan's career started in 1987, when Wales were dealt a humiliating defeat in the World Cup semi-finals at the hands of the All Blacks. He was captain of the side throughout the disastrous World Cup campaigns of 1991 and 1995, but he always captained the side with dignity and honour and showed a desire to win, which many around him seemed to have lost.

Evans played in three World Cup Finals, scoring a total of seven tries, which put him equal fourth in the try-scoring rankings with only Rory Underwood, David Campese and Gavin Hastings above him.

GRANT FOX
New Zealand

At the first World Cup in 1987, the much-fancied All Blacks had a little-known and inexperienced fly-half winning only his second cap. By the end of the tournament, Grant Fox had become a household name. Scoring no fewer than 52 times, including 30 conversions and 21 penalties, he became the tournament's highest points scorer with 126 – a figure unsurpassed in the last two tournaments.

He was not the most naturally gifted or fastest rugby player, not as strong in the tackle as some of his team-mates or opponents, but he made up for these 'weaknesses' with a superb brain and a coolness under pressure that frequently made him a match winner. He was a perfectionist and a master tactician, able to plan and execute move that often confused or frustrated his opponents. As fly-half for th Blacks in two World Cup campaigns, he was the brain behind t pack, delivering well-timed passes and perfectly flighted kicks to all corners of the pitch.

In all, Fox played 46 Tests for his country and amassed an outstanding 645 points at an average of more than 14 points a game. With a total of 170 points in World Cup Finals, he is ranked third in the all-time point-scoring rankings.

GAVIN HASTINGS
Scotland

From an early age, Gavin Hastings had the mark of greatness stamped upon him. He was captain of the first Scotland schoolboys' side to win on English soil, and he captained the victorious Cambridge University side in the 1985 Varsity match against Oxford. It was as player and more recently as captain of Scotland and the British Lions that he became a household name. An uncompromising, hard-tackling full-back, he made surging, high-knee-kicking charges out of defence, kicked towering conversions and penalty kicks, and gave the game everything he had.

We'll have another knees-up when we've won.

For a big man, he was fast over the ground and his size gave him the power and stature rarely seen in a back. He used his power to amass a point-scoring record, kicking goals from the touch-line and sometimes even from within his own half. In the World Cup of 1995, he kicked nine penalties in the match against Tonga, equalling the world's best tally at international level. In that same tournament, against Ivory Coast, he scored four tries, two penalties and no fewer than nine conversions for a personal points tally of 44.

In 61 matches for Scotland, he scored 17 tries, 86 conversions and 140 penalties, for a points total of 667 – an all-time British record. Hastings remains the highest points scorer (227) in the history of the World Cup. He is also the third-highest try scorer in Finals history, with nine.

RALPH KEYES
Ireland

Not the most celebrated individual, Keyes's main claim to fame was his performance in the 1991 World Cup, where his kicking propelled his country through the first-round matches into a mighty quarter-final confrontation with Australia. He was close to putting Ireland in the semi-finals too. Having already scored a total of 54 points in the first three games, including all 15 points in the encounter with Scotland, Keyes' magical boot kept Ireland in touch with the Aussies for most of the match. With only five minutes remaining, his three penalties and a drop goal meant Ireland trailed by only 12-15. When Gordon Hamilton scored Ireland's only try of the match, Keyes's touch-line conversion gave Ireland an unexpected lead. Then, David

Campese and Michael Lynagh combined to give Australia the lead in the last few seconds and snatch a 19-18 win.

Keyes was the highest points scorer in the 1991 World Cup. His 68 points included two drop goals (the only two he attempted) and 16 penalties, and his 23 points in the match against Zimbabwe was also a record for the tournament.

Despite being a superb place-kicker and a very accomplished fly-half, Ralph Keyes played very few times for his country. He gained only eight caps for Ireland but is still the eighth-highest scorer in Irish rugby history with 94 points.

FRANCOIS PIENAAR
South Africa

It was only the ban on South African teams competing in international tournaments that prevented Francois Pienaar from occupying centre stage at more World Cups. He was an outstanding example of the modern rugby player. Tall and powerful, he was a mobile flanker, equally adept at running with the ball or destroying the opposition with timely and effective tackles. His all-round play in the close encounters of scrums, rucks and mauls was excellent, as was his ball handling at the line-out and on the run.

Although he played only 29 Tests for South Africa, he was captain in all of them including, of course, the famous victory against New Zealand in the 1995 final.

The perfect role model for all aspiring young rugby players, Pienaar was just as influential off the pitch as he was on it. During the World Cup, he became the figurehead of the entire tournament, effectively becoming the South African ambassador for sport long before his country ended the competition in such triumph.

WERE YOU PAYING ATTENTION?

Here is a simple quiz to find out if you have taken in all the information in this book. Instead of telling you the answers to all the questions, we have given you the number of the page where you will be able to find out if you got the answers right.

		Page
1.	Who are the current rugby world champions?	20
2.	Who are the current rugby sevens world champions?	45
3.	Who are the current rugby Olympic champions?	69
4.	Who did New Zealand beat in 1995 with a World Cup Finals scoring record?	82
5.	Who did Japan beat 134-6 in the Asian zone of the 1999 World Cup qualification process?	24
6.	How many grounds are being used in these World Cup Finals?	16
7.	How many points will be awarded to a team that loses a match in the Finals?	10
8.	Which two teams contested the only drawn game in World Cup Finals history?	76
9.	In which country was French full-back Serge Blanco born?	86
10.	Which Scottish wing scored five tries in the recent qualifying match against Spain?	30
11.	Who was top points scorer in the 1991 Finals?	81
12.	Who scored the winning drop goal in the 1995 final?	83

MAKE YOUR OWN RUGBY WORLD CUP PREDICTIONS

Use your skill to select the teams that you think will win each of the groups and progress through the tournament to the final. After the final have another look at what you predicted to see how well you did.

POOL MATCHES

	The winner will be	The runner-up will be
A	....	....
B	....	....
C	....	....
D	....	....
E	....	....

The best third-placed team will be ....

Give yourself 10 points for every correct position and 5 points if you got the right team, but in the wrong position.

The four semi-finalists will be

....

....

....

....

Give yourself 20 points for every correct team.

The champions will be ....

The runners-up will be...

Give yourself 25 points for each correct answer and 10 points if you predicted the right finalists but the wrong winner.

The top points scorer in the tournament will be.................................

The top try scorer in the tournament will be.................................

Give yourself 30 points if you get either of these people correct.

Now count up how many points you have got. The maximum is 300. If you got anywhere close, you can consider yourself an expert.

Well done!

SELECT YOUR DREAM TEAM

When the action has finally died down, select your own 'dream team' from the 300 players who were on display in the 1999 World Cup Finals.

MY WORLD CUP DREAM TEAM

POSITION	PLAYER	COUNTRY
Prop	....	....
Hooker	....	....
Prop	....	....
Lock forward	....	....
Lock forward	....	....
Flanker	....	....
Flanker	....	....
Number 8	....	....
Scrum-half	....	....
Fly-half	....	....
Wing	....	....
Centre	....	....
Centre	....	....
Wing	....	....
Full-back	....	....